Contents

▌Words appearing in the text in bold, **like this**, are explained in the Glossary.

Steroids – what's the deal?

Some people are tempted to take steroids because they think the drugs will improve their sporting performance. Others take them because they feel bad about their appearance and think that steroids will help to change it. However, the drugs don't always work in the way people think they will. They can have harmful effects on the mind and body, as Peter, an amateur **body builder** aged 24 from Texas in the United States, found out.

▌ Large, naturally toned muscles can take a long time to build up. Some people may use steroids because they think they will provide a short cut, but steroids are not a healthy choice.

Peter was desperate to change his body shape so he'd feel more confident. He started training at a local gym, but became frustrated when the results weren't happening quickly enough. He began to hang around with people who used steroids, and they persuaded him to try them. He'd heard some rumours about the bad **side effects** these drugs can have, but his friends told him they were safe. He didn't know many facts about steroids, but thought they might work for him. Within a few weeks, Peter collapsed at home after a dizzy spell, and ended up in hospital.

"I thought I had to make myself physically perfect. Perhaps then people would like me, admire me, and think I was attractive. I was willing to do whatever it took to reach my goal. They gave me bad advice. They said steroids and other drugs were the only way to achieve the body shape I wanted. I had never experimented with drugs before and I trusted them. Now I understand they didn't know what they were talking about.

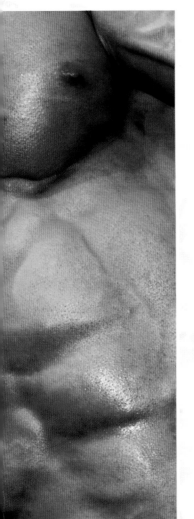

"After I woke up in hospital I realized I had been given a second chance. The drugs and the lies all had to stop. I took a long look at myself, and made a commitment to enjoying a healthy, drug-free life."

What would you have done if you were Peter? One day you may be offered steroids by someone you know. Do you know what you would say?

Making decisions

This book will give you the information you need to make your own decision about steroids. It looks at why some people are tempted to use them. It lays out all the risks to a person's body, mental health, and appearance.

There are many issues to think about. Why are we so obsessed with appearance and winning at all costs? What are the safest, healthiest ways to look and feel good? Let's look at steroids and find out about the real harm they can do.

What are anabolic steroids?

Anabolic steroids are made of chemical substances called **hormones**. Some anabolic steroids are hormones that occur naturally in the human body, such as **testosterone**. Others are drugs that are made **synthetically** (artificially) in factories.

Are all steroids the same?

Anabolic steroids should not be confused with other steroids, such as **corticosteroids**. Corticosteroids are a type of steroid that can occur naturally in the body. They are also made synthetically to treat a number of medical conditions, such as arthritis (inflamed, painful joints) and asthma (a condition that makes breathing difficult). People often use the word "steroids" to refer to both anabolic steroids and corticosteroids. For the rest of this book, the only kind of steroids we'll be looking at will be anabolic steroids.

! Street names for anabolic steroids

Street names for steroids include: roids, juice, and gear. They are also known by brand names such as Winstrol, Deca-Durabolin, Depo-Testosterone, or Equipoise.

Natural anabolic steroids

Small amounts of anabolic steroids are made naturally by the human body. In males, the main **sex hormone** is testosterone, which is a type of anabolic steroid. Testosterone is made in the testicles in males. Smaller amounts of this hormone are also made by the **adrenal glands** just above the kidneys in both males and females. Males normally have much higher levels of testosterone than females. The amount of testosterone that boys produce increases during **puberty**.

Testosterone has two major effects – it makes the human body more masculine and it promotes the growth

Question

What are hormones?

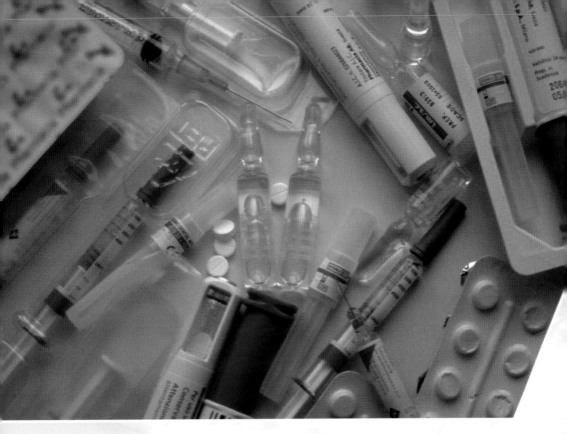

■ There are many different kinds of anabolic steroid drugs. They usually come in tablet form or as a liquid that is injected.

of muscle tissue ("anabolic" means "building up"). You can read more about the effects of testosterone on the body on pages 8–9.

Synthetic anabolic steroids

Synthetic anabolic steroid drugs are available legally only to someone who has a **prescription** signed by a doctor. Anabolic steroid drugs have similar effects to natural testosterone. They have some medical uses (see pages 10–11), but they are also **abused** by some sportspeople and others who think these drugs will help to improve their performance or change their appearance. Abuse of anabolic steroids can lead to serious health problems.

Hormones are chemical substances that are made in special **glands** inside the body. They are carried round the body in the blood and help to control the levels of certain substances in the body.

How do anabolic steroids work?

All anabolic steroids act in a similar way to the male **sex hormone testosterone**. They promote the growth of muscle tissue in the body and increase the body's male characteristics. To look at how anabolic steroid drugs work in the body, it is useful to look at the normal actions of testosterone.

Testosterone and male characteristics

Testosterone is responsible for many changes that happen to boys during **puberty**. Puberty is the time when a series of physical and emotional changes take place that make children develop into adults. In boys, puberty usually takes place between the ages of ten and eighteen years. During this period, the male sex organs develop and become mature and the person becomes physically capable of reproducing.

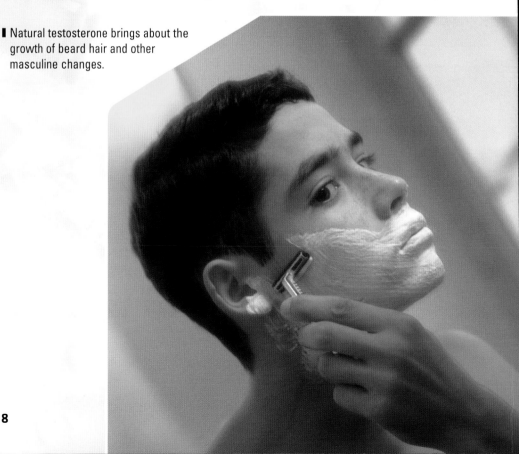

❚ Natural testosterone brings about the growth of beard hair and other masculine changes.

During puberty, testosterone also causes the development of **secondary sexual characteristics**. These are physical changes that make a boy's appearance more masculine or "manly". They include:

- growth of a beard

- growth of thicker, darker body hair

- tissue growth in the larynx (voice box) that causes the voice to deepen or break, and a visible **Adam's apple** at the front of the neck

- slight changes in body shape

- subtle changes to the shape of the face

- coarsening of facial skin.

⚠ Discovering testosterone

The **hormone** testosterone was first discovered in 1935. It was found by some Dutch scientists who were experimenting on bull testicles. Later that year, researchers gave testosterone to some dogs, and found that it increased the size of their muscles under certain conditions. By the late 1930s, it was being given to patients who were not able to produce enough of their own testosterone.

Testosterone and growth

Testosterone is released into the bloodstream from the testicles and the **adrenal glands**. When combined with exercise and a high protein diet, it has the effect of increasing the body's ability to use protein to make muscle tissue. Testosterone can also stimulate the **bone marrow** to make more red blood cells. Red blood cells carry oxygen to the muscles, which improves the performance of the muscles. Slight increases in the amount of testosterone in the body influence the growth of long bones (the arms and legs) in teenagers. The shape of the body also changes, with a slight increase in the amount of muscle, broadening of the shoulders, and a slight decrease in the amount of body fat. All this means that a boy's weight can double between the ages of ten and eighteen.

Anabolic steroids do have some approved medical uses, but doctors are very careful about how they **prescribe** these drugs and only use them to treat a few patients with certain medical conditions. They are used to treat people who can't make enough of their own **testosterone**, and to help certain patients recover from weight loss or muscle wasting following an injury or long period of illness.

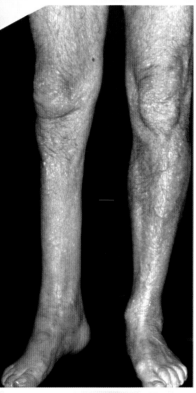

I Doctors sometimes give steroids to patients who have muscle wasting after illness or injury. The steroids help the patient to regain muscle.

Replacing natural testosterone

A few males are unable to produce enough natural testosterone, so doctors may give small amounts of anabolic steroid drugs to increase the levels of this **hormone** to normal. When teenage boys do not produce enough testosterone, they may suffer from delayed **puberty**. A doctor can perform tests to find out the reason for the delayed puberty. If it is because of low testosterone levels, they can give anabolic steroids to help bring on the changes that testosterone causes, such as beard growth and the voice breaking. Anabolic steroids are also sometimes given to older men who stop producing their own testosterone. This is known as **replacement therapy**. When doctors prescribe anabolic steroids to replace testosterone, they give the drugs in tiny amounts – just enough to restore the levels of the hormone to normal.

Wasting and weight loss

Very small amounts of anabolic steroids are also used to help some patients who have serious muscle wasting or general weight loss. This can happen after long periods of bed-rest after surgery. The anabolic steroids help to speed up recovery, and rebuild muscle tissue. They may also be given for short periods to people who are suffering from severe **malnutrition**, to help them regain weight.

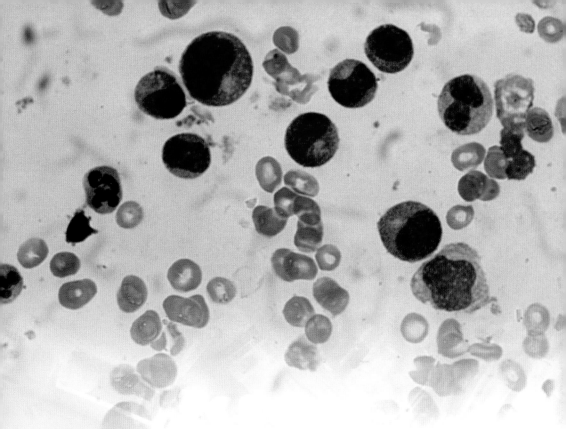

A rare form of anaemia

Anaemia is a condition in which there are not enough healthy red cells in the blood. Red cells deliver vital oxygen to all the tissues of the body, so when there are not enough healthy red cells the body's tissues do not get sufficient oxygen. There are many different kinds of anaemia. Anabolic steroids are sometimes used to treat aplastic anaemia, in which the **bone marrow** does not produce enough blood cells.

Careful supervision

When doctors treat patients with anabolic steroids, they are very careful to prescribe the correct dose. They also monitor the patients closely to make sure they are benefiting from the treatment and not suffering from unwanted **side effects**. When people **abuse** anabolic steroids, they may take over a hundred times the recommended amount that doctors use to treat patients. This greatly increases the risks to their health.

❚ This picture, taken with a special microscope, shows the blood of a patient suffering from aplastic anaemia. There are far fewer red blood cells (the small grey cells in the photo) than normal. The larger cells in the picture (coloured blue here) are white blood cells.

11

Anabolic steroids and the law

In most countries, there are strict laws about anabolic steroids and people need a signed **prescription** form from a doctor before they can buy or use these drugs. Selling steroids illegally, or giving them away, can lead to a fine or prison sentence. Sporting organizations around the world also have strict rules about drugs and have banned the use of anabolic steroids.

Anabolic steroid laws

In the United Kingdom, the law classes anabolic steroids as Class C drugs, along with drugs such as cannabis and some **amphetamines**. They are also classed as "prescription only" drugs. This means that they can only be legally issued by a **pharmacist** to a person who has a prescription signed by a doctor. It is not against the law to possess small amounts of anabolic steroids, unless the drugs have been made illegally. However, possession of larger amounts or sharing the drugs with a friend is classed as **supply** or **dealing**, and can be punished by up to fourteen years in prison plus an unlimited fine.

I At airports, customs officers often search people's bags for drugs. If someone is caught with a large amount of steroids in their possession, they may face a prison sentence.

I After Ben Johnson won the 100-metre final at the 1988 Olympics, he tested positive for steroids. He was stripped of his medal and was banned from competitions for two years. In 1993 he was banned for life after another positive test.

In Australia and New Zealand, it is illegal to possess or supply steroids without a prescription. Penalties include fines of between Aus$2000 (£800) and Aus$100,000 (£40,000) and prison sentences of up to 25 years.

Sporting organizations

Sporting organizations have banned the use of several substances including anabolic steroids. This is because these drugs might enhance a sportsperson's performance artificially and pose serious risks to their health. Sportspeople are regularly tested to see if they have banned substances in their bodies. If someone is caught cheating, he or she will be thrown out of a competition and may be banned from taking part in future competitions.

Viewpoints

Some people think that stricter laws and harsher penalties would be the best way to stop steroid abuse. Others disagree.

- **The law should be stricter and penalties harsher**
Making the law stricter and giving people harsher penalties would mean that people would be less likely to sell and buy illegal steroids. It would also put people off trying them, because they would be more scared of being punished.

- **Stricter laws would not stop people taking illegal steroids**
Making punishments harsher would not stop the illegal sale of steroids. It would be more effective to improve education about these drugs, and help people who have body image problems. There should also be more emphasis on helping people give up steroids.

What do you think?

Anabolic steroid abuse

Most young people never try anabolic steroids, but steroid **abuse** has increased among certain groups of people over the last few years. So who abuses these drugs and what is it that makes people try them?

⚠ Steroid statistics

- In the United Kingdom, surveys of male students aged 16 to 19 suggest that up to 4 per cent of them have tried anabolic steroids at least once.

- Studies show that males are slightly more likely to try steroids than females, and teenagers make up between one third and half of all steroid users.

- Most teenagers who try steroids only take them once or twice.

Steroid abuse in sports

Steroid abuse started in the late 1940s among people in power sports, such as weightlifting and throwing events in athletics. It quickly spread to a large range of sports including tennis, baseball, and swimming. Nowadays, despite being illegal in many countries and banned in most sports, steroids are taken by certain people throughout the sporting world.

Some sportspeople, both amateur and professional, may be tempted to try anabolic steroids because they are under pressure to improve their performance and they think steroids will help them. This pressure may come from friends, team members, or even sports coaches.

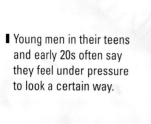

❚ Young men in their teens and early 20s often say they feel under pressure to look a certain way.

▮ Most people say no to steroids. Taking regular moderate exercise is one of the best ways to be naturally fit and healthy.

These people take steroids because they think the drugs will help them increase their muscle size and strength more quickly and enable them to train harder and longer. But there are many risks that come with taking steroids – these drugs lead to harmful changes in the body that are hard or impossible to reverse. You can read more about the effects of steroids on sporting performance on pages 18–19 of this book.

Who else abuses steroids?

Most people do not use steroids, but some studies suggest that between 5 and 40 per cent of regular gym users may be on steroids. Many of these people are **body builders**. There may also be increased use among people who have been abused and bullied, people with body image problems, and people with "tough guy" images such as security guards and nightclub door staff.

Many of these people think that steroids will help to change the way they look. In particular, they may want to increase the size of their muscles so they look more "masculine". They may be disappointed to find out that the drugs can have unpleasant effects on their looks. You can read more about these effects on pages 32–33 of this book.

Are we obsessed with the way we look?

As we have seen, some people take anabolic steroids because they think the drugs will change the way they look or help them achieve a certain body shape. Why do so many people feel under pressure to change their appearance like this?

In the 1950s, curvy actresses such as Jane Russell used to be thought of as the most glamorous women.

Young people and body image

During the teenage years, young people have to cope with natural changes in their body shape, and they also want to fit in with their friends and be considered attractive. This pressure can play a part in eating disorders such as **anorexia** and **bulimia**. It can also make some people try unhealthy diets or drugs such as anabolic steroids.

Changing fashions

Young people may also feel under pressure to achieve a certain body shape because a particular type of appearance is in fashion. However, appearances that are fashionable today would perhaps have been considered unattractive in the past. In the 1950s and 1960s, the most popular and glamorous actresses were pear-shaped or "curvy". Male actors were often square-chinned and barrel-chested, and did not have as much muscle tone as many actors do today. Throughout the 1980s, exercise classes and gyms became more popular. Many of the women seen in the **media** were thinner than in the past and many of the men were more muscular.

In the 1990s, many advertisements used waifish, skinny women, or boyish-looking men as models. It was also the time of supermodels who were all tall, very thin women. Less than 1 per cent of people in the world have a body type like supermodels.

Different body shapes go in and out of fashion, but people come in all shapes and sizes. Today's fashionable appearances are impossible for most people to achieve.

A false impression?

If you look at a picture of a celebrity, it has usually been shot under very flattering lighting. After the picture has been taken, the image is nearly always re-touched to hide spots, scars, wrinkles, and dark circles under the eyes. Re-touching can even make people look slimmer, more muscular, or taller. In films, body doubles (other actors or models) are often used to create a false impression about an actor's body. Celebrities often have lots of money to spend on their appearance. Unlike most people, they can easily afford cosmetic surgery, a personal trainer, a nutritionist, a make-up artist, and a stylist. It's completely unrealistic for a normal person to try to look like them.

⚠ Reverse anorexia

Reverse anorexia is a condition in which someone thinks their muscles are much smaller than they really are. Men with reverse anorexia think they're weak or puny, and women think they're flabby, even though they are fit and toned. People with this condition may be more likely to abuse steroids.

❙ In the 1980s, the actor Arnold Schwarzenegger became known as a leading action hero and was famous for his large, well-toned muscles. However, it is completely unrealistic for most men to look like this.

Steroids and sporting performance

Some people take steroids and other substances because they think this will give them an advantage in sports competitions. **Performance-enhancing drugs** do not always help people win, but most people agree that using them is cheating.

What are performance-enhancing drugs?

Performance-enhancing drugs, including anabolic steroids, are substances that some people take because they think they will improve their performance in sports and help them to win competitions. Most of these substances are banned by sports organizations, usually because they give sportspeople an unfair advantage or because they may be harmful to their health.

Can steroids make someone a better athlete?

To be a top athlete, a person needs to practise, learn skills and techniques, have good coordination, and develop speed, strength, and endurance (stamina). Steroids may give an athlete a slight advantage with some of these things. However, steroids have no effect on performance unless someone trains hard and has a good diet at the same time. Most experts agree that these drugs help people recover faster after exercise. This means that people can train harder before an event and be better prepared.

Some scientists also believe that steroids increase muscle size and perhaps strength, when combined with training. These effects give sportspeople who use steroids an advantage over other athletes who rely on their natural sporting ability and hard

▌ Hungarian weightlifter Ferenc Gyurkovics won a silver medal at the 2004 Olympics, but was later disqualified after failing a drugs test.

training. However, if someone is not a good athlete in the first place, steroids are unlikely to help them win competitions. The drugs also have many health risks and harmful **side effects**. You can find out more about these health risks on pages 26–39.

THG

THG (tetrahydrogestrinone) is a banned steroid drug that has only recently been created. For a while, organizations that carry out drug testing in sports competitions didn't know this drug existed, and it didn't show up in tests. This is because it was specially designed by its creators not to show up in tests – a so-called "**designer steroid**". Tests have now been developed that can detect it. Designer drugs are only made and sold illegally and they have never been tested for their safety. This means that little is known about their effects. There is no way to tell if they truly improve performance or not, or what their side effects and risks might be.

Hundreds of different products are on sale in health food stores and gym shops, aimed at people who do sports and work out, or who are trying to lose weight. They are sold as "**supplements**" or "**training aids**". Most of these are harmless in small amounts, but some supplements have strong effects and can be harmful to health. This group includes **andro**, ephedra, creatine, and **diuretics**. Many of these supplements have recently been banned by governments or sporting organizations.

Training aids and supplements

Nowadays, the shelves in health food shops are piled high with training aids and dietary supplements. Many of these products claim to help with **body building** or weight loss. Some of these products, such as protein drinks, simple snacks, and vitamins, are harmless when taken in small amounts. Other training aids and supplements have drug-like actions, and can be risky to use.

Health risks

Just because a product is on sale in a health food store, that doesn't mean it's "healthy". Manufacturers often try to encourage customers to buy these products by labelling them "natural", "legal", or "steroid-free". However, they can in fact be very harmful to a person's health. Supplements may sometimes cause allergic reactions, or they may interfere with medications. Sometimes, people who **abuse** steroids take a mixture of training aids at the same time. This is sometimes described as "**stacking**". Mixing different drugs or supplements together greatly increases the risks of using them.

Are supplements legal?

In the United States, the United Kingdom, and many other countries, there are no government controls on

Jenna's story

Jenna, a student aged nineteen, bought some supplements at a health food shop because she thought they would help change her body shape. They were labelled "natural", and she thought they would be completely safe. But they had unexpected effects.

"Just last week I had a really bad reaction to some supplements. I was shaking and my heart was racing and I felt like I was going to have a heart attack. I was sweating and I could not breathe. I blacked out three times. It was so bad I could hear my heart beat in my ears."

the sale of many supplements. However, some supplements (such as andro) that are legal to buy are converted into banned substances such as **nandrolone** after they get inside the body. This means that sportspeople who are tested for banned substances would fail the test if they had used these supplements.

❚ Although some supplements and training aids are safe, many are dangerous and their use is banned in certain sports.

Andro and DHEA

Andro (short for androstenedione) and **DHEA** (dehydroepiandrosterone) are chemicals that are widely sold as **supplements**. These chemicals are also produced naturally in small amounts by the human body, and can be changed into **testosterone** or other **sex hormones** by reactions inside the body. It is thought that this also happens to andro and DHEA once they get inside the body, so they are likely to have the same performance-enhancing effects and the same risks and **side effects** as anabolic steroids. Many sporting organizations have banned the use of andro and DHEA, but they are legal to buy.

Ephedra

Ephedra (also called Ma Huang) is a herbal substance that has a **stimulant** effect. It increases the heart rate, and can lead to people pushing themselves too far physically. Ephedra can cause heart attacks and fits (seizures), and several deaths have been linked to its use. The sale of ephedra is restricted in the United Kingdom and it is illegal in the United States.

▮ Some people feel they're under pressure to win at any price and they may think training aids and supplements will help them.

▮ Although the packaging looks scientific, there is very little scientific knowledge about many supplements.

Creatine

Creatine is a substance naturally found in foods such as beef, tuna, and pork. It is also made in small amounts in the human body. However, creatine is also sold as a supplement in powder or capsule form. It may help a person's performance in sports that need fast bursts of energy, such as weightlifting or sprinting. Creatine can have very unpleasant side effects, including nausea (feeling sick), vomiting, muscle cramps, diarrhoea, unwanted weight gain, and dehydration.

Diuretics

Diuretics are drugs that increase the amount of urine a person produces. Steroid **abuse** can lead to people's bodies holding on to too much water, and some users take diuretics to get rid of this extra fluid and reduce their bloated appearance. Strong diuretics can make people suffer from confusion and cramps, and sometimes they make people collapse.

Viewpoints

Many supplements on sale in health food shops have not been tested for safety. Some people think supplements should only be put on sale if they have been proven to be safe. Other people disagree.

● **Supplements should be sold only if they have been proven to be safe**
Some supplements have serious health risks, but they are widely available to buy. Manufacturers should be forced to test the safety of all supplements. Those that are found to have health risks should be taken off the shelves.

● **There's no need to test all supplements**
Most supplements are not dangerous. Many are herbs that have been used for centuries. It's unrealistic to expect manufacturers or governments to test them all because it would cost too much money.

What do you think?

23

What's in illegally bought steroids?

When people buy anabolic steroids illegally, there's no easy way to tell what they're getting. Some of these drugs may be **counterfeit** drugs, or fakes. They may have been manufactured illegally and contain all kinds of harmful substances.

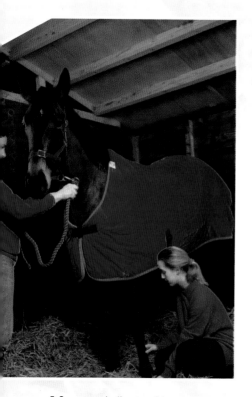

▌Some anabolic steroids are stolen from vets, and are only suitable for use on large animals such as horses.

Where do these illegal steroids come from?

Anabolic steroids that are offered for sale illegally come from a number of different places. Some may have been stolen from hospitals, clinics, or factories. Others may have been bought legally in countries that allow over-the-counter sales of steroids in **pharmacies**, without the need for a **prescription**. The drugs are then transported into another country illegally. Some illegally sold steroids may be old, out-of-date stocks that should have been destroyed. Others may have been stolen from vets, and are designed only for animals. Drugs that are meant for large animals come in doses that are much too high for humans.

Illegal manufacture

Many drugs sold illegally as anabolic steroids are fake or counterfeit. These fake drugs are usually made in illegal factories or laboratories. While some may contain anabolic steroids, many often contain no anabolic steroids at all. Fake drugs are often sold in packaging that makes them look like real medical supplies. This means that counterfeit drugs are sometimes very hard to spot.

Using illegally manufactured drugs can be very dangerous. For example, it is impossible to know the dose contained in these drugs, so the amount taken may be much higher than someone was expecting. The drugs are made under illegal and unhygienic conditions. This means they may be contaminated with all kinds of harmful bacteria, mould, or poisonous chemicals. Sometimes anabolic steroids are mixed with chalk, paracetamol, milk powder, or glucose sugar. This bulks them out, so the **dealer** makes more profit. Counterfeit capsules have also been found to contain dirty water and vegetable oil.

A note about drug dealers

People who sell anabolic steroids illegally may try to persuade others that they are providing a helpful service and that the drugs they are selling are completely safe. However, they are mainly selling the drugs to make money. This is their real motivation. Some of them also give dangerous "advice" about what drugs to take and how to take them – this is often so they can sell more of the drugs. This advice is not based on anything scientific – their so-called "knowledge" is often based on guesswork and rumours, passed from one person to another.

❙ Illegally made drugs tend to be created in very unhygienic situations. They may contain bacteria and other toxic substances.

How do anabolic steroids affect a person's health and what damage can these drugs do to the body? When people **abuse** steroids, they often take amounts that are many times higher than medically recommended doses. This has serious health risks – it can affect the heart, brain, liver, kidneys, and overall health. People who abuse anabolic steroids also risk damaging their joints, muscles, and bones through **over-training**.

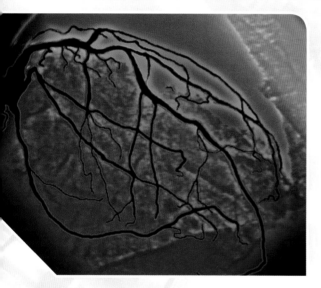

▌ This picture shows the arteries in a healthy heart. Steroid abuse can raise levels of cholesterol, which makes these arteries clog up.

Risks to the heart and blood vessels

Anabolic steroids can damage the heart and blood vessels in several different ways:

■ The drugs raise the levels of a type of **cholesterol**, and this fatty substance can clog up a person's arteries. This increases the risk of heart disease, heart attacks, and chest pain. It can also lead to a **stroke** (when the blood supply to part of the brain is cut off, often causing disability or death).

■ Steroids also increase the chance of **blood clots** forming in a person's blood vessels. Sometimes blood clots are pumped up into the heart, lungs, or brain, which can kill or cause serious illness.

■ Steroid abuse may also cause the heart to become enlarged, so it has difficulty pumping blood around the body.

❚ Steroid abuse may lead to high blood pressure, which can cause many health problems.

Risks to the liver and kidneys

Steroid abuse can also be harmful to the liver. Steroids quickly damage the liver cells, but this damage can usually be reversed if a person stops taking the drugs. Anabolic steroids can cause a rare illness in which blood-filled sacs form inside the liver. There is a risk that the sacs may burst and cause internal bleeding. People who use steroids in large amounts may also have an increased risk of liver cancer or kidney problems.

Risks to general health

Anabolic steroid abuse doesn't just damage the heart, liver, and kidneys. People who abuse steroids often suffer from other more general health problems. A person who abuses steroids may find that they have swollen **glands** (also called lymph nodes) in their neck, armpits, and groin after taking the drugs. They may catch colds and flu more often than other people. They may suffer from headaches, nosebleeds, stomach pains, and a flushed (red) face. Steroid abuse can also lead to sore throats, sore tongue, and bad breath.

27

The risks of over-training

Professional athletes and sportspeople all know that rest
is part of a successful training programme. It helps the body
to recover from the strains of exercise, and is good for
general health. Some people who **abuse** anabolic steroids
spend long periods doing sports training or working out at
the gym. They often train and work out for longer hours
than other people, or they may train every day of the week
without a rest break. They may also push themselves too far
physically, straining their muscles, or lifting weights that are
too heavy for them. This **over-training** can lead to all kinds
of injuries, as well as pains in the muscles and joints, and a
greater chance of catching colds and flu.

Hard exercise routines with lots of
repetitive movements can cause
tiny breaks in the bones called
"stress fractures". These
are painful and need
medical attention,
followed by weeks
of rest. Exercising
too hard and
gaining weight
because of muscle
growth can put lots
of strain on the
joints, sometimes
leading to
osteoarthritis
(deformed, painful
joints, and loss
of mobility).

❙ Training too hard can
damage bones, joints,
muscles, and tendons.
These injuries can be
very painful and may
make taking part in
sports impossible.

Steroids and bone growth

Did you know that anabolic steroids can stop teenagers from growing to their full natural height? Areas near the ends of long bones are slightly soft in teenagers, allowing the bones to keep growing. Steroids make these soft areas of bone become tougher and hardened, which means that the normal teenage "growth spurt" doesn't happen properly. This is a permanent change, and users can end up shorter in height than they should be. Tendons, the fibrous tissues that join the muscles to the bones or steady certain joints, can also rupture (break) because they are weakened by steroid abuse.

▌ Under the influence of steroids, some people lift weights that are too heavy for them, leading to injuries.

Risks to the immune system

It has recently been shown that after a few weeks of steroid abuse, the **immune system**, which protects the body against infections, can be damaged. Steroid abuse can cause a special kind of white blood cell called a "natural killer" cell to stop working properly. These cells normally destroy viruses or early cancer cells. This effect can happen even if someone is using very tiny amounts of anabolic steroids.

"Steroids have a seriously detrimental [harmful] effect on a specific part of the human body's immune system. Anyone taking steroids over a long period of time ... is seriously endangering their health."

Dr Robert Weatherby, sports science expert, Southern Cross University, New South Wales, Australia

What do anabolic steroids do to your skin?

Anabolic steroid **abuse** can be very bad for a person's looks. It increases the risk of getting bad acne spots, **stretch marks**, and a whole range of other skin disorders.

Steroids and acne

If someone has acne, they may have a mixture of blackheads, whiteheads, and pustules (zits or spots). It is well known that anabolic steroids may cause acne to appear, and if a person has acne already, steroids can make it many times worse. When acne is really bad, there's a risk that spots will leave permanent scars on the skin. The affected areas of skin tend to be mostly on the face, back, and chest. Severe acne from steroid abuse is often hard to treat and takes a long time to clear up. Sufferers may even develop cysts under their skin surface. These are sacs containing fluid or semi-solid material. They are often painful, needing medical attention, and may leave scars.

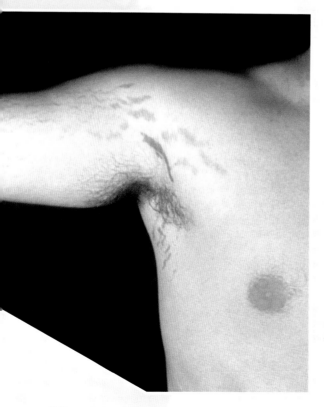

Steroids and stretch marks

Stretch marks are fine lines that appear on the body when a layer of tissue (called the dermis) gets torn underneath the surface of the skin. This can happen when someone abuses steroids because the skin is stretched too much owing to rapid weight

❚ Steroid abuse can lead to rapid increase in muscle bulk, which can cause stretch marks in the skin.

30

gain or change in muscle size. New stretch marks are reddish or purplish, and they fade over time to leave silvery or pale flesh-coloured marks. There is no effective way to remove these marks.

Other skin problems

There can be other problems too. Steroid abuse can cause an increased risk of developing general skin irritations, rashes, and itching. When taken in large amounts, anabolic steroids can also lead to bruising of the skin. People who abuse steroids may get bruising after minor injuries, but bruising can also occur when the skin has not been injured at all. Steroid abuse also leads to an increased risk of developing hives. This is a condition in which a person develops red, swollen itchy marks all over their body. In severe cases, hives can be fatal, so medical care is needed.

▌Steroids often cause new acne to appear, or make existing acne much worse.

❗ Sex hormones and acne

Anabolic steroid drugs behave like **testosterone** when inside the body. When they are abused, these drugs are often taken in very high doses, so the testosterone-like effects can be very strong. Natural testosterone makes oil **glands** in the skin produce more oil. Anabolic steroid abuse also acts in this way and makes the skin become more greasy. When more grease is produced, dead skin cells and other dirt are more likely to get trapped in the pores of the skin, and acne bacteria begin to grow there too. The result is blocked pores and spots.

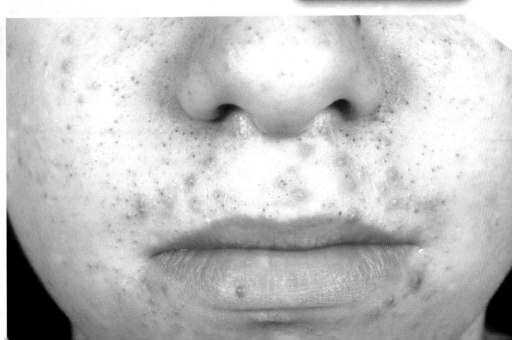

Some men who **abuse** steroids think these drugs will make them more masculine and "manly". In fact, there are several ways in which steroid abuse can have the opposite effect. Taking large amounts of steroids can also lead to difficulty in passing urine and it can make young men go bald.

The male reproductive system

Large doses of steroids eventually make the body shut down its own natural production of **testosterone**. A lack of this natural **sex hormone** can lead to a reduction in the amount of sperm a man produces, making him less fertile (less able to father a child). A lack of natural testosterone can also cause the testicles to shrink in size. A man's sex drive may decrease and he may lose all interest in sex. Some men who abuse steroids lose their ability to get or keep an erection. All these effects are usually reversed when someone stops taking anabolic steroids.

Effects on the prostate gland

Use of anabolic steroids can make the **prostate gland** swell up. This can cause difficulty or pain when passing urine. Some experts suggest it can also lead to an increased risk of prostate cancer.

Steroid abuse and baldness

Many men (and a few women) are born with a genetic (inherited) tendency to lose their hair, usually from the top and sides of their head.

❚ Anabolic steroid abuse causes early baldness in many young men.

▌Taking drugs is not part of a healthy lifestyle. There are lots of ways for young people to stay fit without taking drugs.

This is called "male pattern baldness". Anabolic steroid abuse speeds up this process, so instead of losing their hair in their 50s or 60s, someone who abuses steroids may end up with a bald patch or thinning hair in their teens or 20s.

Growth of breast tissue

Did you know that men who abuse steroids run the risk of developing breasts? This is because steroid abuse can lead to the production of a female sex hormone called oestrogen in males. Having a lot of oestrogen in the body can cause lumps of breast tissue to grow under a man's nipples. These lumps never go away, even if someone stops taking steroids, and can only be removed by surgery, which tends to leave scars.

Anabolic steroid **abuse** has many effects on the bodies of women and girls, often giving them a more "manly" appearance. The drugs can also affect a woman's periods, or cause harm during a pregnancy and afterwards.

I Steroid abuse may lead to many changes in the female appearance, making them appear more masculine.

Question

Are the changes that steroids cause in females permanent?

Steroids and female appearance

Just as natural **testosterone** affects a boy's appearance and voice during **puberty**, anabolic steroid abuse in women and girls may cause changes that make them appear more masculine or "manly". This includes growth of thicker, darker facial and body hair. In some women, steroid abuse even leads to the growth of a moustache and beard. The skin on the face also becomes slightly rougher, and more oily. Sometimes, the tissues around the voice box (larynx) thicken, leading to a deepened voice, similar to a teenage boy's voice breaking during puberty. Some women develop a visible **Adam's apple** at the front of the throat. Breast tissue can shrink dramatically and the breasts can sag. These changes tend to make a female body appear less traditionally feminine, which can cause problems or embarrassment for some users.

Steroids and the female reproductive organs

Taking high doses of male **sex hormone**-like drugs can disrupt the delicate balance of **hormones** inside the female body. In particular, it can cause changes in the menstrual cycle (cycle of periods). Periods may become irregular and in some women, the periods may stop altogether. This may make it very difficult for them if they want to become pregnant.

The risks of steroid abuse during pregnancy

Healthy pregnancy involves a fine balance of many hormones, including sex hormones. Steroid abuse may cause an increased chance of miscarriage, where the pregnancy fails before the baby is due to be born. There may also be a greater risk of stillbirth, where the baby is born dead. Some experts also think that there is more chance of birth defects, where live babies are born with something wrong with them. This includes female babies being born with genitals that have a male appearance, and babies of either sex being born with other physical problems.

▌Anabolic steroids may harm a developing baby, whatever the stage of pregnancy.

Anabolic steroid **abuse** doesn't just affect someone's body and appearance. It can also have serious effects on their mental health. Anabolic steroids can affect concentration, and may cause restlessness, anxiety, and depression. It can take a very long time to recover from these problems, as steroids often linger on in the body for months after a person stops taking them.

Steroids and behaviour

Some steroid users experience changes in their behaviour and mood while they are taking the drugs. They may become over-confident, and think they are more important than the other people around them, or

▌Steroid abuse can lead to irritability and outbursts of aggression.

Martha's story

When someone abuses steroids, it doesn't just affect their own life. Martha, a mother of three teenage children, found that when her eldest son began to abuse steroids his behaviour changed dramatically and it affected the whole family.

"My son's steroid use has ruined my life. He has become violent, flies into rages, and doesn't care who he hurts in his obsession to get bigger and stronger. He is frightening. A very caring and sweet young man has turned into a monster. Think about what usage of this stuff does to the other people around you. This is a drug like any of the others. Just because you look more fit, does not mean you are healthy. I live in constant fear that he will hurt me, his sister, someone else, and himself."

wrongly start thinking they are unbeatable. They may also feel more driven to train hard at the gym, which can lead to harmful amounts of strain on their bodies. Many users find they have difficulty concentrating on things, and find it hard to focus attention on important tasks.

Some experts believe that steroids can also lead to mood swings, aggression, strong feelings of jealousy, sexual violence, and domestic violence. This is sometimes referred to as "**roid rage**".

Can steroids make you feel unhappy?

Steroids can make people more irritable than usual, and a significant proportion of users say that they have difficulty sleeping because of steroids. Others suffer feelings of anxiety or panic. Steroids may also make users feel **paranoid**, when they feel as though someone or something is "out to get them" or trying to harm them. Steroids may also lead to depression in some users, where they feel very down for long periods. This tends to clear up after they stop taking the drugs, but steroids stay in the body for a long time, so improvement may take a while.

Why is injecting so dangerous?

Anabolic steroids are sometimes taken as tablets, but many people inject them into their bodies with a needle. People who inject their bodies with steroids are putting themselves at particular risk. Injecting steroids can cause a number of problems, including tissue damage and life-threatening infections.

! HIV

HIV stands for Human Immunodeficiency Virus. Once inside the body, this virus gets into special blood cells (called CD4 cells) that are part of the **immune system**, and stops them working. This means that the body starts to lose its ability to fight all kinds of different infections and certain cancers that it can normally kill off. This can eventually lead to AIDS (Acquired Immune Deficiency Syndrome). At the moment there is no true cure for HIV or AIDS.

Damage from injecting

When someone injects anabolic steroids (or what they think are anabolic steroids), the needle can easily damage their body tissues. Some people end up with scars, or inflamed and painful nerves. Steroids prepared for injection are meant to be injected directly into a muscle. If the drugs are injected into a vein or artery by mistake, it can cause serious injury and even death. Injecting steroids puts any impurities the drugs contain straight into the body's tissues. Some of these impurities can make people very ill.

Infections

When people inject steroids, they use a needle to break through the natural protective surface of the body. Bacteria that may live harmlessly on the skin can cause all kinds of problems if they end up inside the body. For example, they can cause pain and abscesses (collections of infected pus) at the injection site. Bacteria can also cause blood poisoning.

If users share needles, an infection from the blood of one person can be put straight into the bloodstream of the other person. In this way, life-threatening infections, such as **HIV** (the virus that can lead to AIDS) and **hepatitis B** or **C** (which can cause damage to the liver), can easily pass from one person to another. Many people who are infected by these diseases seem to be perfectly healthy and normal, and they may not realize they are infected for a long time. However, they can still pass the infection on to others.

Using dirty or shared needles and syringes can also lead to a condition called infective endocarditis. This illness is an inflammation of the inside of the heart and its valves, and it can be fatal.

❙ When someone injects steroids, their body tissues can easily be damaged and harmful bacteria can enter their body.

Dependence is when a person has an unhealthy habit that they feel unable to give up. This habit could be anything from smoking cigarettes to gambling or drinking too much alcohol. Can people become dependent on steroids?

Becoming dependent

Many people who **abuse** steroids tell themselves they'll only use them for a short period of time. But people who abuse steroids can become dependent on the drugs. This can make it hard for users to stop taking steroids, even though they know that these substances have many health risks and may be causing them serious problems. You can read more about giving up steroids on pages 42–43.

Psychological dependence

Some people who abuse steroids go on to develop mental or **psychological dependence** on the drugs. Some people who use steroids regularly start to think that they cannot function properly without taking the drugs. Others keep taking the drugs to avoid the feelings they have when they stop taking them and their body goes back to normal. Users who stop taking anabolic steroids may also have **cravings**, in which they have a strong desire to take more drugs.

As dependence develops, it can take over a person's life, until the drugs become the most important thing in it. Users who are dependent on steroids often ignore the health risks of the drugs and continue to use them, in spite of their **side effects**.

Many people who are dependent on steroids spend a lot of time and money trying to get the drugs. But dependence doesn't just drain people of their money, it can also harm personal relationships and badly affect a person's education or chances of getting a good job.

Question

What is psychological dependence?

Signs of dependence

Signs that someone is becoming dependent on steroids include a person:

- thinking about the drugs more and more, or worrying about where the next lot is coming from

- lying about drug use or becoming angry when challenged

- feeling bad about the drugs, but unable to stop using them

- missing school or work because of drugs

- continuing to use drugs, in spite of the physical, emotional, relationship, work, or money problems they are causing

- feeling unhappy after coming off the drugs, and taking more to avoid these feelings.

▍Dependence can creep up unexpectedly, and it can make someone's life a misery.

Answer

Psychological dependence is when someone feels they cannot cope with everyday life without a drug. They come to rely on the drug because of the way it affects their emotions and their moods.

41

There are many reasons why people who **abuse** steroids decide to stop. They may be experiencing unpleasant **side effects** from the drugs, or they may have serious concerns about the health risks associated with using them. They may also decide they want to achieve their ambitions naturally, without the help of drugs. Some people who abuse steroids may be able to give them up without too many problems, but others need more help.

Physical effects of giving up steroids

When someone decides to stop taking anabolic steroids, their body goes through some changes as it returns to its natural healthy state. The person may lose a little muscle, and probably some extra water too. This process takes a few days or weeks. Some users do not feel any ill-effects at all, but others may have temporary discomfort. They may suffer from tiredness or disturbed sleep for a while, for example. A few people have problems with headaches, muscle and joint pain, loss of appetite, flu-like chills, or feeling sick. These problems tend to pass within a few days.

Mental effects of giving up steroids

Some users feel a little restless, down, irritable, or lacking in energy for a while after stopping the drugs. A few people become very low and depressed after giving up, and they may suffer from these feelings for a long time. When people feel depressed, a doctor may need to treat them for a few months or sometimes longer.

❚ Giving up steroids is a step towards a more positive healthy lifestyle.

Some people, who were originally drawn to steroids because they feared looking weak or vulnerable, find it very hard to cope with loss of muscle. Others worry that they will not be able to cope without the drugs and that their sporting performance will be badly affected. But they should soon find that they are able to do perfectly well by themselves.

"I'm just getting off steroids. Hell is the word I think of when you say steroids. Depression, disturbed sleep, you're lucky if you get three or four hours of sleep a day."

Aaron, a student aged nineteen

Getting help

Most steroid users are able to stop using the drugs on their own, or with the help of a sympathetic family doctor who can give them a health check and moral support. There are also drug helplines, which people can call for advice (see pages 54–55). Many towns have drug clinics, and users may benefit from talking through their difficulties with trained **counsellors**, or joining support groups.

▌Family doctors or drug counsellors can be great sources of help to people who want to stop taking steroids.

Individuals, sports organizations, schools, and governments all have to work together to tackle the problem of steroid **abuse**. The supply of the drugs needs to be reduced, but so too does the demand for them.

Reducing the supply and demand

Police forces and customs officers work hard to reduce the supply of illegally sold drugs. In many places, specially trained police officers are employed to find and arrest drug **dealers**, and shut down illegal factories that make **counterfeit** or fake drugs. **Pharmacists** also help to cut down the supply by looking out for fake or stolen **prescriptions**.

To help cut down demand, government departments, health services, schools, and youth organizations provide information about drug issues, and get people talking and thinking about the subject. But most importantly, individual people have to educate themselves about healthy lifestyles and the true risks of steroids.

Zero tolerance

Some schools try to prevent drug abuse by operating a "zero tolerance" policy. This means that any pupil who is caught using drugs or with drugs in their possession will be automatically punished. In some schools, a pupil is given a warning for a first offence, or they may

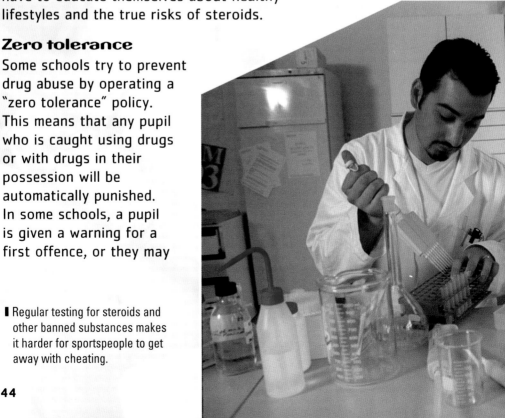

❙ Regular testing for steroids and other banned substances makes it harder for sportspeople to get away with cheating.

be temporarily suspended from school. However, in other schools pupils may be immediately expelled. Some people think that taking harsh action helps to reduce drug abuse. Others argue that a better approach is to offer **counselling** and education about drugs while allowing the students to stay in school.

Making it harder to cheat

Drug-testing organizations get better and better at catching drug cheats every year, even though new drugs are being created all the time. Testing organizations are also developing ways to detect newer "**designer steroids**" (see page 19).

Viewpoints

Some people think that testing secondary school students for drugs, including anabolic steroids, will help to reduce drug abuse. Others disagree.

- **Drug testing is an effective way to stop drug abuse**
Regular drug testing in secondary schools sends out a clear message to students that drug use is wrong. If students know they're likely to get caught, they may be less likely to try drugs. Regular testing may also help former users to stay drug-free.

- **Drug testing is not the best way to prevent drug abuse**
A very strict approach is likely to make students rebel and they may turn from illegal drugs that would make them fail the test to heavy alcohol use, which is also dangerous. The money spent on drug testing would be better spent on treating people with drug problems and educating young people about drugs.

What do you think?

Taking some pride in your appearance and looking after your body can be very positive. If you don't feel good about the way you look, there are lots of healthy things you can do to feel better.

How to look your best

People don't need illegal drugs, complicated fitness regimes, or expensive products to make the most of their appearance. In fact, most of the best tips are simple, and are either free or very cheap:

- Eat a healthy diet most of the time. For the average person this means lots of fresh fruit and vegetables, wholegrains, lean meat, and fish (or vegetarian alternatives), and a little dairy produce. Keep desserts, chocolate, and other sugary foods for occasional treats. The same goes for fried food and junk food.

- Drink plenty of water, especially in hot weather.

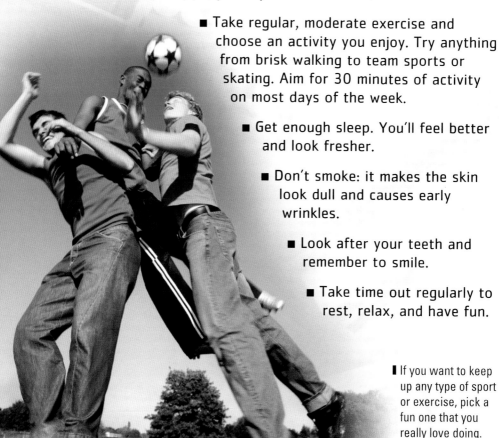

- Take regular, moderate exercise and choose an activity you enjoy. Try anything from brisk walking to team sports or skating. Aim for 30 minutes of activity on most days of the week.

- Get enough sleep. You'll feel better and look fresher.

- Don't smoke: it makes the skin look dull and causes early wrinkles.

- Look after your teeth and remember to smile.

- Take time out regularly to rest, relax, and have fun.

▌If you want to keep up any type of sport or exercise, pick a fun one that you really love doing.

!Feeling bad about your looks?

Remember, you don't have to be covered in muscles or super-skinny to be attractive.

Make a list of all your best points and ask good friends to add to the list. Friendly? Funny? Smart? Kind? Most good qualities are nothing to do with looks.

If you're still feeling down, try talking to a **counsellor** or your doctor. They can show you lots of ways to feel better about yourself. By developing good habits now you can make positive changes to your body.

▋A healthy lifestyle does not include quick fixes. Regular exercise can lead to positive, lasting changes.

Changing the way we look

If you want to lose weight, see your family doctor first. He or she can weigh you properly to see if you're really too heavy, and will offer you advice about sensible diets and exercise if you need it. If you want to get fitter, it can be helpful to work out a realistic fitness programme with someone at your local sports centre. If you want to feel stronger and more confident, try something like self-defence classes or martial arts. It can be tempting to look for shortcuts, but getting fit or losing weight slowly and naturally is much better. It will leave you feeling great, with long-lasting results and no negative **side effects**.

It's up to you to make healthy choices in your life, even though there are times when you will feel it's difficult. Anabolic steroids are not a shortcut to success or an attractive appearance, and they can lead to many health and legal problems.

Anabolic steroids are not a healthy choice

Steroids and similar drugs can be bad for your health, looks, mental state, and relationships. A drug arrest can lead to time in prison, ruin a future career, and prevent travel to some countries. If you want to look your best, there are lots of healthy ways to do this without taking drugs. If you want to be a go-getter or a big success at something, you need a positive attitude and motivation, not chemicals.

❚ Most people who play sports feel that taking part is more enjoyable than trying to win at any cost.

Under pressure?

Drugs might seem like an easy solution if you are desperate to win. But cheating undermines the whole idea of a fair competition. Cheats can also be found out, shamed, and banned. If people you know are using drugs, you don't have to copy them to fit in. Real friends will never try to force you into taking steroids. If your sports coach puts you under pressure to take drugs, they are breaking the law. In this situation, it's best to talk to someone such as a parent or a teacher at school.

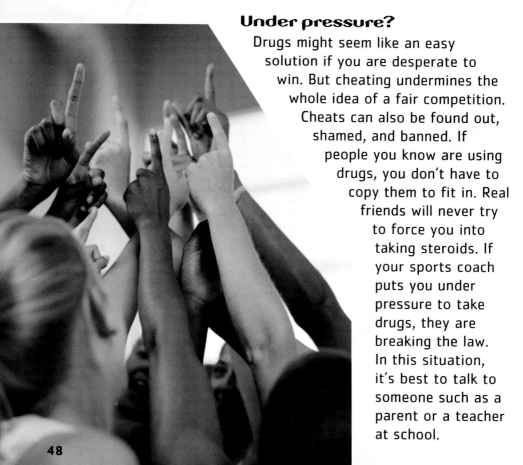

Chris's story

Chris is a **body builder** who does not use steroids. He believes they are definitely not part of a healthy lifestyle.

*"I don't take anything that changes my **testosterone** levels. That's why I'm natural. I want to be the guy that's 65 years old and still lifting weights and competing and still into fitness. I'm in it for the long term. I've worked in a gym, and I can tell you there have been numerous individuals that I've known over the years who have died. Some of them have committed suicide because of the mental aspects of using steroids."*

Thinking ahead

One day you might be offered steroids, and it's good to be prepared and think over what you'll say in advance. Remember:

- simply saying "no thanks" or "I'm not interested" is usually enough

- if someone keeps bothering you, say "no thanks" over and over again

- change the subject and talk about something else

- if they won't stop, walk away from the person

- there are telephone numbers to call and sympathetic people you can talk to

- it's your life – nobody can tell you what to do and it's up to you to make your own decisions.

▍Working together as part of a team can help to build up friendships and self-confidence, as well as helping you to get fit.

Do you want to know more about steroids, or are you worried about somebody who might be using drugs? There are many people and organizations who can give you the right information.

Finding out more

If you want to find out more about anabolic steroids and the problems associated with them, you may want to start by looking at booklets or leaflets about drugs. Your school or college, or local health or youth centre, may have printed information available. Your town or school library may also have books about drugs.

You can also find out more information from one of the many organizations, groups, and charities that provide information and advice about anabolic steroids and other drugs. Many of these organizations have useful websites and some supply information packs.

Someone to talk to

Sometimes it can be hard to talk to people you know about the things that are worrying you. You may want to discuss your concerns **in confidence**, knowing that whatever you say won't be passed on to anyone else. You may also feel you need some expert advice. Many organizations run telephone helplines staffed by specially trained advisers. Some of these helplines are open 24 hours a day, so you can call them for advice and information whenever you like. You don't have to have a drug problem yourself to call. You will find details of these organizations and helplines on pages 54–55 of this book.

Question

If I talk to the doctor, will they tell my parents?

Worried about someone else?

If you're worried about someone else's drug use, you don't need to bottle your feelings up and try to cope on your own. There are places you can go for help and support.

I It might seem difficult to call a helpline, but the staff are trained professionals who know how to help in all kinds of situations.

You may find it helpful to call a helpline. It may also help to talk to a **counsellor**, your family doctor, a school nurse, or a teacher at school. In this sort of situation it's common to feel that you're the person who is responsible for keeping family secrets, or that you have to cover up for your friends when someone is in trouble. This can be very stressful and it is always better to talk about it, if possible.

Answer

Most doctors or nurses will talk to teenagers in confidence. However, doctors do have to tell parents if they think a patient is too young to understand what's happening, or if they think an adult is taking advantage of a teenager.

Glossary

abuse use of drugs for non-medical reasons in a way that has a bad effect

Adam's apple part of the throat that sticks out. It contains the voice box and is particularly prominent in men.

adrenal gland small gland found just above the kidneys. Adrenal glands make several different hormones, including testosterone.

amphetamine type of stimulant drug that speeds up the activity of the brain

anaemia medical condition in which there are not enough healthy red cells in the blood

andro shortened name for androstenedione, a supplement that can have steroid-like effects

anorexia eating disorder in which a person has a distorted impression of their own body and a strong desire to lose weight even though they may be very thin

blood clot semi-solid lump that forms inside a blood vessel

body builder person who does special exercises to increase the size of their muscles

bone marrow soft fatty tissue inside the centre of large bones. It produces blood cells.

bulimia eating disorder in which a person regularly binges on large amounts of food, and then gets rid of the food by vomiting or exercising

cholesterol waxy, fatty substance found in certain foods and the blood. Some types are linked to heart disease.

corticosteroid form of non-anabolic steroid that helps reduce inflammation in the body

counsellor person trained to give advice and guidance to people to help resolve their problems

counterfeit something that is a copy or a fake, not the real thing

craving strong or uncontrollable need or longing

dealer person who buys and sells drugs illegally

dependence when a person is unable to cope without a drug

designer steroid steroid that has been deliberately developed to avoid detection in drugs tests

DHEA shortened name for dehydroepiandrosterone, a supplement that can have steroid-like effects

diuretic drug that increases the amount of urine someone produces

gland organ inside the body that releases liquid chemicals such as hormones

hepatitis B and **C** infections caused by a virus that can seriously damage the liver

HIV virus that can lead to AIDS

hormone substance made in glands that changes the way certain cells behave

immune system group of white cells and tissues that protect the body from infections

in confidence privately, without telling anyone else

malnutrition physical weakness and bad health caused by general lack of food, or lack of certain essential substances in food

media TV, cinema, magazines, and newspapers, and any other form of mass communication

nandrolone anabolic steroid that is produced naturally in the human body in tiny amounts and is also made synthetically

over-training exercising too energetically or training for too long

paranoia feelings of suspicion and distrust and a sense that everyone is out to get you, or to criticize your behaviour or actions

performance-enhancing drug drug that gives someone an unfair advantage in sport. Most of these substances are banned by sports organizations.

pharmacist trained person who prepares and dispenses drugs

prescribe to write an instruction (a prescription) that authorizes a medicine to be issued to a patient

prescription instruction written by a doctor that authorizes a medicine to be issued to a patient

prostate gland gland found around the neck of the bladder in males

psychological dependence when a person feels they need drugs to get through everyday life and cannot cope without them

puberty when a person moves from childhood into adulthood

replacement therapy treatment involving small amounts of hormones, such as testosterone, being given to increase levels back to normal

roid rage slang term for aggressive outbursts caused by anabolic steroids

secondary sexual characteristics physical characteristics that develop during puberty and distinguish males from females but are not involved in reproduction

sex hormone steroid hormones, such as oestrogen and testosterone, that affect the growth and function of the reproductive organs, and the development of secondary sexual characteristics

side effect unwanted effect of a drug or medical treatment

stacking slang term for taking a number of drugs and/or supplements at the same time

stimulant drug that speeds up the activity of the brain, making people feel alert and full of energy

stretch marks fine lines that appear on the body when a layer of tissue gets torn underneath the surface of the skin

stroke sudden change in the blood supply to part of the brain. It can cause loss of physical functions such as movement or speech.

supplement substance that is added to the diet, in the hope of improving it

supply give or sell drugs to other people illegally

synthetic made artificially using chemicals

testosterone main male sex hormone

THG (tetrahydrogestrinone) synthetic steroid that was designed to avoid detection in drugs tests carried out by sporting bodies

training aid commercial product taken by some sportspeople and body builders who are trying to improve their performance

Contacts and further information

There are a number of organizations that provide information and advice about drugs. Some have helpful websites, or provide information packs and leaflets, while others offer help and support over the phone.

Contacts in the UK

Adfam
Waterbridge House, 32–36 Loman Street, London SE1 0EH
Tel: 020 7928 8898
www.adfam.org.uk
Adfam is a national charity that gives confidential support and information to families and friends of drug users. They also run family-support groups.

Connexions Direct
Helpline: 080 800 13219 (8 a.m.–2 a.m. daily)
Text: 07766 4 13219
www.connexions-direct.com
This service for young people aged thirteen to nineteen offers information and advice on a wide range of topics, including drugs. Young people can also speak to an adviser by telephone, webchat, email, or text message.

DrugScope
32–36 Loman Street, London SE1 0EE
Tel: 020 7928 1211
www.drugscope.org.uk
A national drugs information agency with services that include a library, a wide range of publications, and a website.

FRANK
Tel: 0800 776600
Email: frank@talktofrank.com
www.talktofrank.com
An organization for young people that gives free, confidential advice and information about drugs 24 hours a day.

Narcotics Anonymous
UK Service Office, 202 City Road, London EC1V 2PH
Helpline: 020 7730 0009 (10 a.m.–10 p.m. daily)
www.ukna.org
A fellowship of people who have given up narcotics, using a twelve-step programme similar to the one used by Alcoholics Anonymous. They have a helpline for users and their friends and relatives, plus events and meetings around the United Kingdom.

Release
Helpline: 0845 4500 215 (10 a.m.–5.30 p.m. Mon–Fri)
Email: ask@release.org.uk
www.release.org.uk
An organization that provides legal advice to drug users, their families, and friends. The advice is free, professional, non-judgemental, and confidential.

Contacts in Australia and New Zealand

Alcohol & Other Drugs Council of Australia (ADCA)
17 Napier Close, Deakin, ACT 2600, Australia
Tel: 02 6281 1002
www.adca.org.au
ADCA works with the government, business, and community organizations to prevent or reduce the harm caused by drugs.

Australian Drug Foundation
409 King Street, West Melbourne,
VIC 3003, Australia
Tel: 03 9278 8100
www.adf.org.au
An organization that works to prevent
and reduce drug problems in the
Australian community.

**The DARE (Drug Abuse Resistance
Education) Foundation of New Zealand**
PO Box 50744, Porirua, New Zealand
Tel: 04 238 9550
www.dare.org.nz
An organization that provides drug
prevention education programmes.

**Foundation for Alcohol and Drug
Education (FADE)**
9 Anzac Street, PO Box 33–1505,
Takapuna, Auckland, New Zealand
Tel: 09 489 1719
www.fade.org.nz
A national organization that provides
services and information throughout
New Zealand.

Narcotics Anonymous
Australian Service Office, 1st Floor,
204 King Street, Newtown, NSW 2042,
Australia
http://na.org.au/
National helpline: 1300 652 820
The Australian division of Narcotics
Anonymous has helplines for users and
their friends and relatives, plus events
and meetings around Australia.

Turning Point
54–62 Gertrude Street, Fitzroy,
VIC 3065, Australia
www.turningpoint.org.au
Helpline (DirectLine): 1800 888 236
Turning Point provides specialist
treatment and support services to
people affected by alcohol and
drug use.

Further reading

*Dr Miriam Stoppard's Drug Information
File: From Alcohol and Tobacco to
Ecstasy and Heroin*, by Miriam
Stoppard (Dorling Kindersley, 1999)

Drugs and You, by Bridget Lawless
(Heinemann Library, 2000)

Drugs: The Truth, by Aidan Macfarlane
and Ann McPherson (Oxford University
Press, 2003)

Health Issues: Drugs, by Sarah
Lennard-Brown (Hodder Children's
Books, 2004)

Just the Facts: Drugs and Sport, by
Clive Gifford (Heinemann Library, 2004)

Teen Issues: Drugs, by Joanna Watson
and Joanna Kedge (Raintree, 2004)

Why Do People Take Drugs?, by Patsy
Westcott (Hodder Children's Books,
2000)

Wise Guides: Drugs, by Anita Naik
(Hodder Children's Books, 1997)

Further research

If you want to find out more about
problems related to anabolic steroids,
you can search the Internet, using a
search engine such as Google. Try using
keywords such as:

Anabolic steroids + risks
Anabolic steroids + laws
Anabolic steroids + dependence
Designer steroids + tests
Drug testing + sport

Disclaimer
All the Internet addresses (URLs) given in this
book were valid at the time of going to press.
However, owing to the dynamic nature of the
Internet, some addresses may have changed or
sites may have ceased to exist since publication.
While the author, packager, and publishers regret
any inconvenience this may cause readers, no
responsibility for any such change can be
accepted by the author, packager, or
publishers.

Index